The Last Cruise of the Cuttlefish

The Cuttlefish was a pirate ship.
It was going home to Parakeet Island.
Molly Mischief was the cabin girl.
Her Aunt Bertha was ship's Captain.

The Cuttlefish was filled with treasure, but there was not much food. Slim Jim, the cook, fed the pirates on ship's biscuit and fish. But the pirates were still hungry. Katnip, the ship's cat, also ate fish.

3

Up in the crow's nest, Tiny, the African pirate, was dreaming of boiled eggs, toast and marmalade, and coffee.

Suddenly he saw a ship.
It was the Skylark, a passenger ship.

The pirate ship sailed up to the Skylark,
and the pirates jumped aboard.
The passengers were terrified.

"We have no gold," said their Captain.

"What have you got to eat?" called Captain Bertha.
"Nothing," said a little girl.
"We ate everything at my birthday party."

The pirates took the passengers as prisoners, and the Cuttlefish set sail for Parakeet Island. The pirates were still hungry and the prisoners were hungry, too. Tiny looked at a chart.

"Not far from here is a bay," he said. "We may find some food there."

Four days later, they reached the bay.
Slim Jim and Molly went ashore in
one of the ship's boats.   Katnip went too.

They found a path through the trees.
Slim Jim called out but no one answered.
As they looked around, they heard a
noise in the long grass.

"Look!" said Molly.   "There's a little dog."
   "That," said Slim Jim, "is a baboon.
Let's get back to the ship."
But they were too late.

Baboons were all around them.
They came out of the long grass
and down from the trees.

The baboons screeched and showed their teeth. Slim Jim swung his cutlass and Molly swung a stick to keep them off.

Katnip ran up a tree to see what was going on. He gave a loud and angry "Miaouw!"

9

Katnip jumped from the tree.
He landed on the head of the
biggest baboon.

The other baboons fled in terror.
Slim Jim and Molly ran fast for the
shore and the boat. Katnip followed.

The pirates cheered when Slim Jim told them about Katnip's brave rescue.

They were all tired of being pirates, so they gave the pirate ship a new name. They called it the Molly Mischief, and they took all the children on a fun cruise.

All Aboard the Molly Mischief

The Molly Mischief was almost ready for the children's fun cruise.
Boys and girls waited to go on board.
Slim Jim and Molly checked the boxes of food.

Katnip was sorry there was no cat food, but he liked fish.

Captain Bertha welcomed the children aboard.
But there was so much noise that no one heard
what she said.

The Molly Mischief sailed out to sea.
The fun cruise had begun.

13

The children chased each other round the deck.
They swung on ropes.   They played tricks on the crew.
They tied Lung Lee's pigtail to a drawer.
They filled Slim Jim's sea boots with water.

At lunch time, Molly rang the bell. "Come and get it!" she called. "Crunchburgers and chips, with Angel Fluff to follow."

"Horrible," said Slim Jim. "The crew will have healthy food." Captain Bertha smiled and said, "Molly is in charge."

After lunch, Pierre was on deck.
Suddenly a girl with a telescope
ran up to Pierre. She pointed out to sea.

"There it is again!" she said.

"What is it?" asked Pierre, as more
children came on deck.

Pierre held the telescope to his eye. "I can't see anything," he said.

Captain Bertha and Slim Jim took turns to look out to sea.
Other people looked too.   No one could see anything.

Captain Bertha looked at Slim Jim.
   "Have you hurt yourself?" she said.
   "No," said Slim Jim.   "Why do you ask?"

17

"Because you have a black eye," replied the Captain.
"You have, too!" said Slim Jim.

They all looked at each other.
They all had black eyes! The children laughed when Captain Bertha saw the black paint on the telescope.

Next morning at breakfast, some children said they were tired of Krispipuffs and Fizzipop. Other children said they did not feel well.

Suddenly there was a loud crash.
The ship leaned over and stopped moving.
Everyone ran on deck.

Water was coming in below deck.
They all grabbed buckets and filled them.
They poured the water over the side.
But the water came in faster than it went out.

Molly asked Slim Jim to get his big soup pot.
They put all the food they had left into the pot.
Slim Jim stirred it and soon it was
thick, sticky and squelchy.

"We've been eating that!" said one of the children.
"Yuk!"

Two sailors carried the pot below.
They put an old sail over the hole in the ship.

Then they poured the sticky mess over it.
The water stopped coming in.

When they got back to land,
the crew mended the hole.
Slim Jim made a marvellous meal of
melon soup, fish pie and a fruit pudding.

The children loved it.
Nobody missed the Choconibbles or Toffocrunch.
They were sorry the cruise was over.

The Dream Ship

I watched a ship put out to sea.
The Captain waved his hat to me.
The sailors sang a sailors' song.
I wished that I could go along.

One day I too will sail away
Where flying fish and dolphins play.
I'll land upon an island shore
Where ripples lap and breakers roar.

There'd be so much I could explore,
I'd stay a week, or two … or more.

(John Grant)